THE
BiBLE
COLORING
BOOK FOR GIRLS

EMAIL US AT

modernkidpress@gmail.com

TO GET FREE GOODIES!

Just title the email
"Bible Coloring for Girls"
And we will send some extra
surprises your way!

Follow us on Instagram!
@modernkidpress

Hello there!

We're so glad you picked up this book!

It is full of hand lettered bible verses with cooresponding illustrations that every little girl will love! We hope that while you find hours of entertainment in these pages you also find inspiration and encouragement through God's Word.

If you have any questions or concerns, feel free to reach out to us at modernkidpress@gmail. com and we will be sure to get back with you.

Happy coloring!

- The Modern Kid Press team

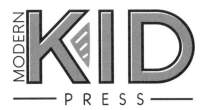

THIS BOOK BELONGS TO:

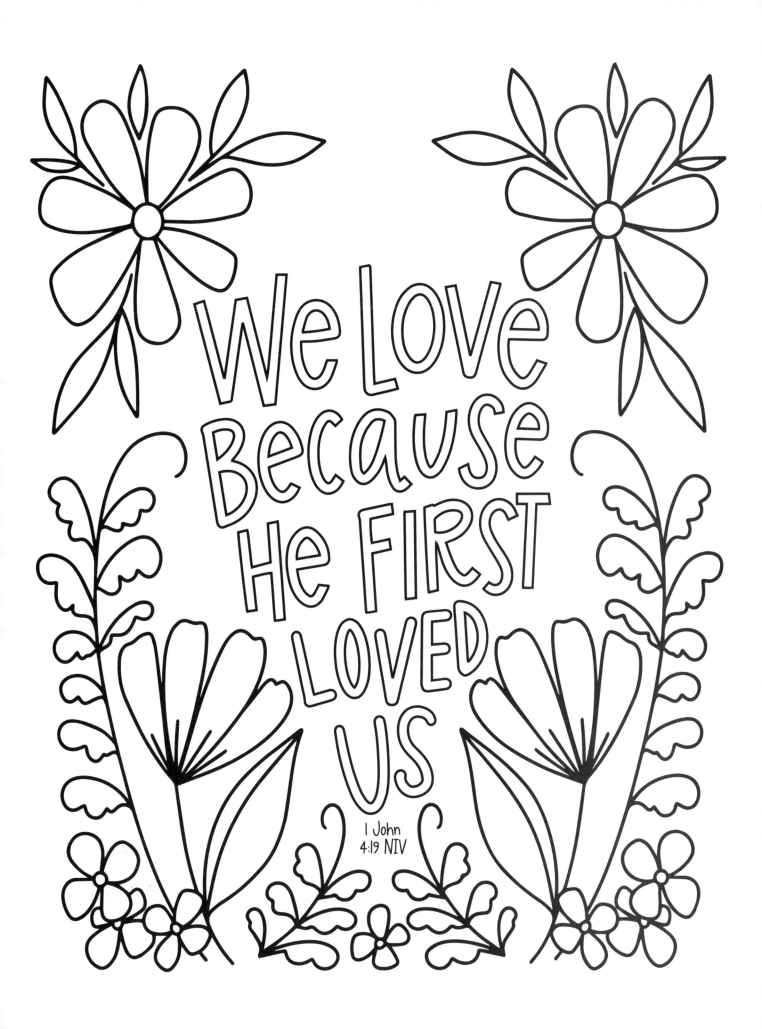

We Love Because He FIRST LOVED US

1 John 4:19 NIV

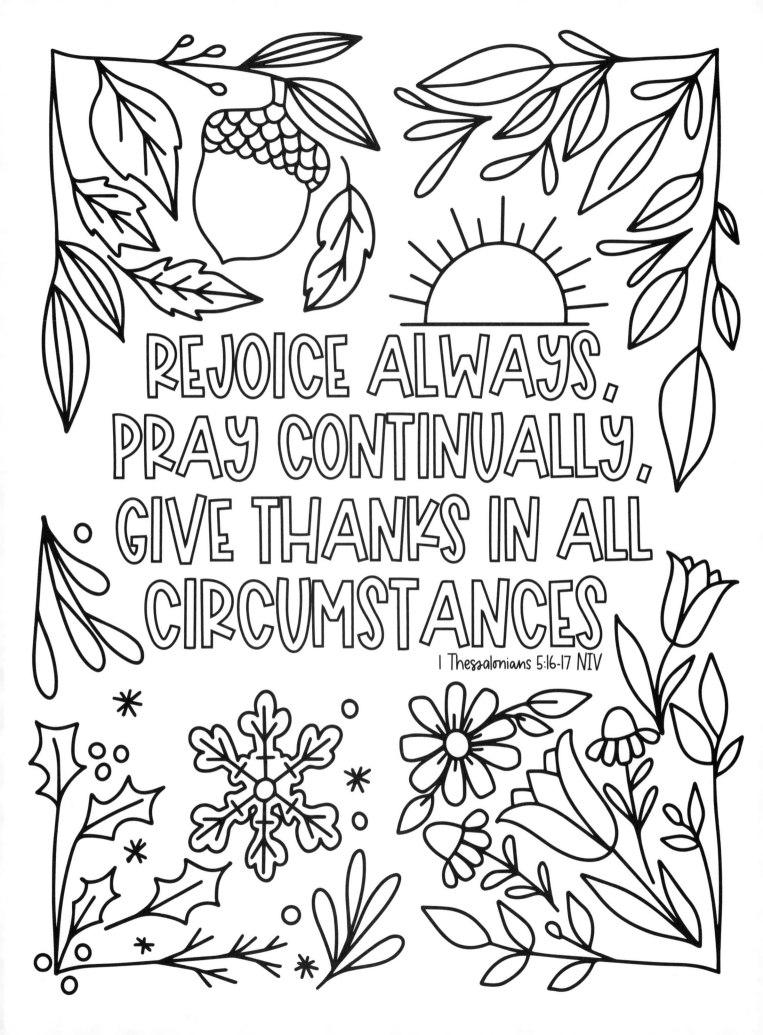

REJOICE ALWAYS, PRAY CONTINUALLY, GIVE THANKS IN ALL CIRCUMSTANCES

1 Thessalonians 5:16-17 NIV

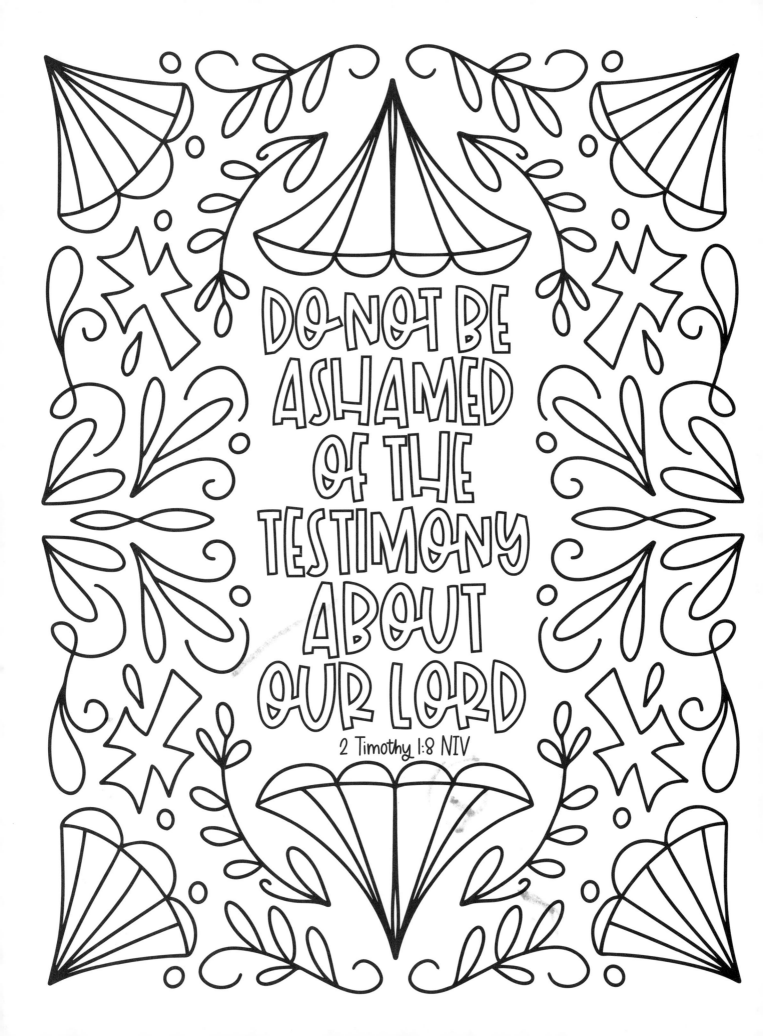

DO NOT BE ASHAMED OF THE TESTIMONY ABOUT OUR LORD

2 Timothy 1:8 NIV

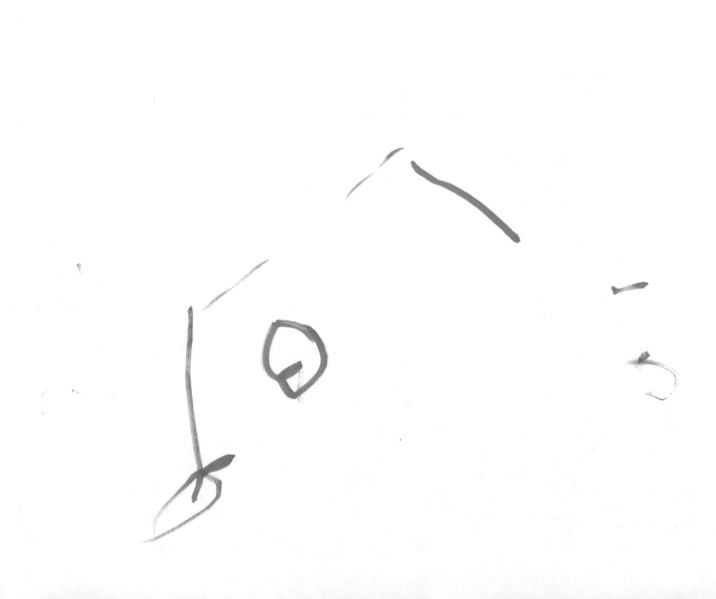

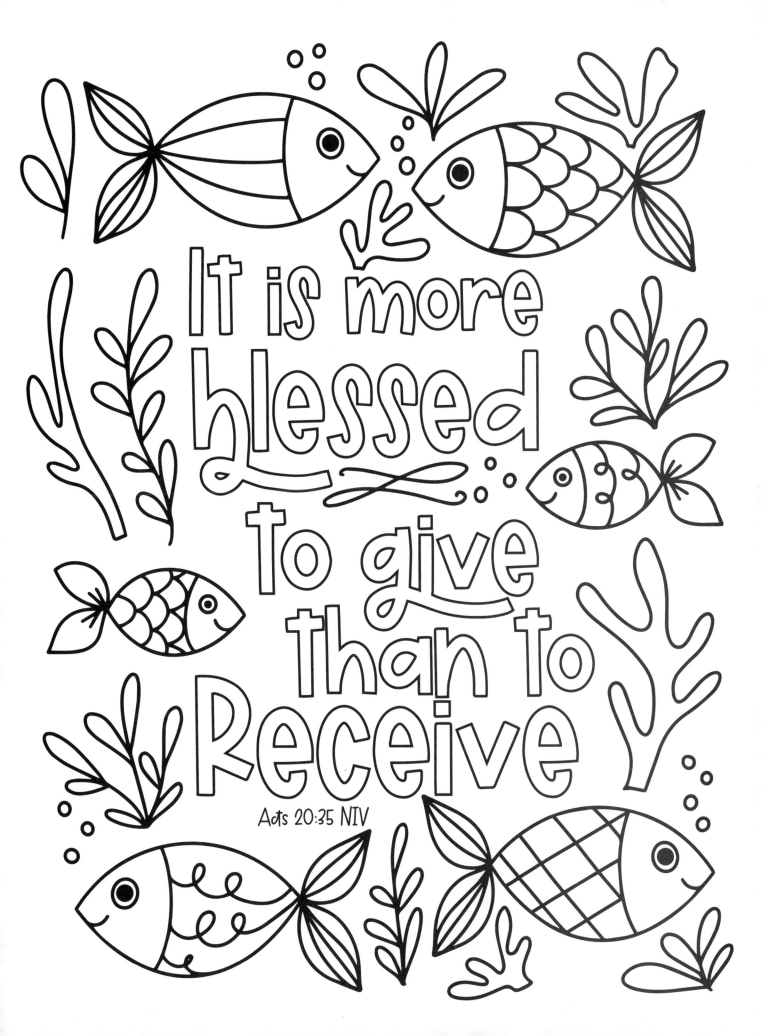

It is more blessed to give than to Receive

Acts 20:35 NIV

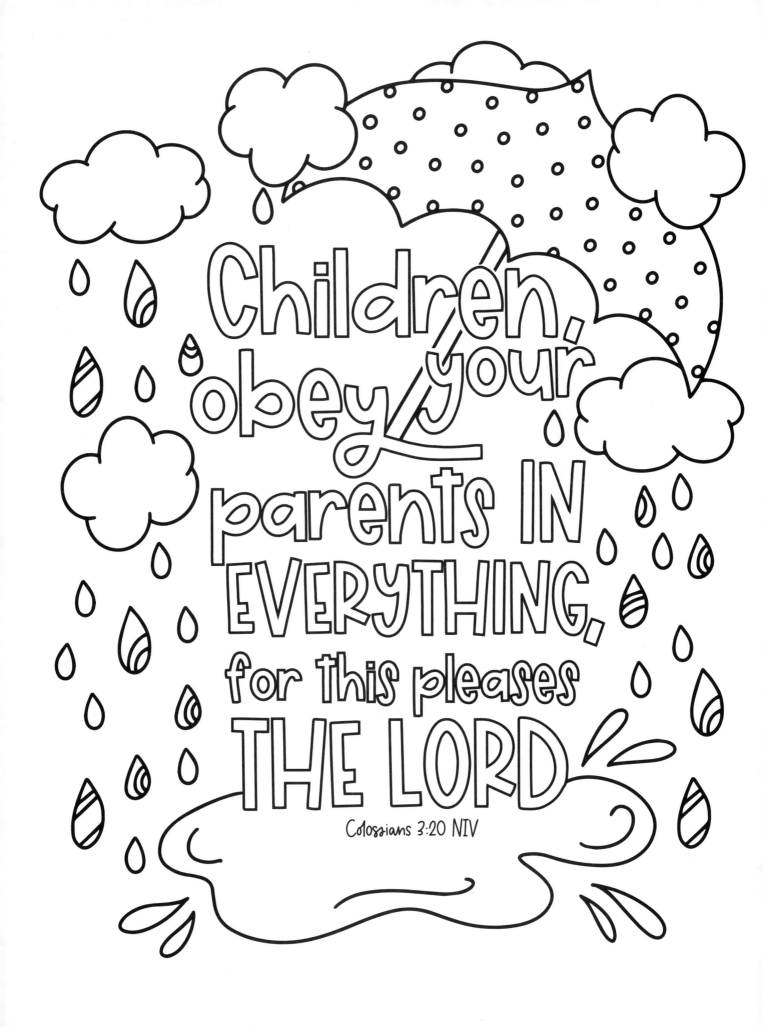

Children, obey your parents IN EVERYTHING, for this pleases THE LORD

Colossians 3:20 NIV

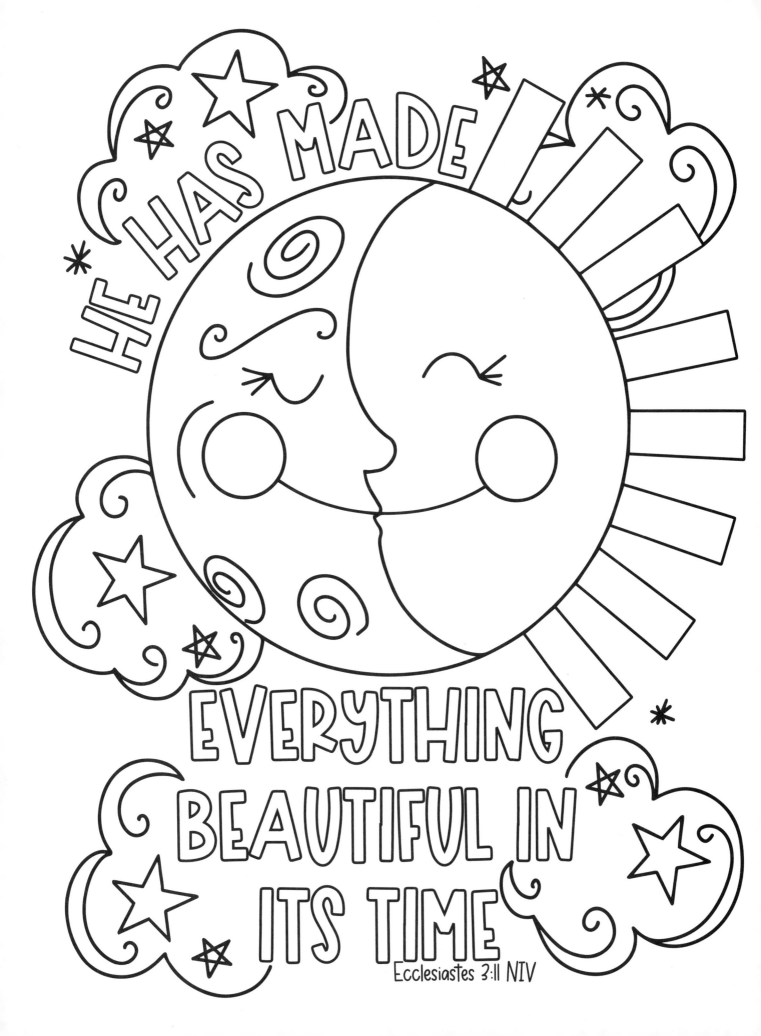

HE HAS MADE

EVERYTHING
BEAUTIFUL IN
ITS TIME

Ecclesiastes 3:11 NIV

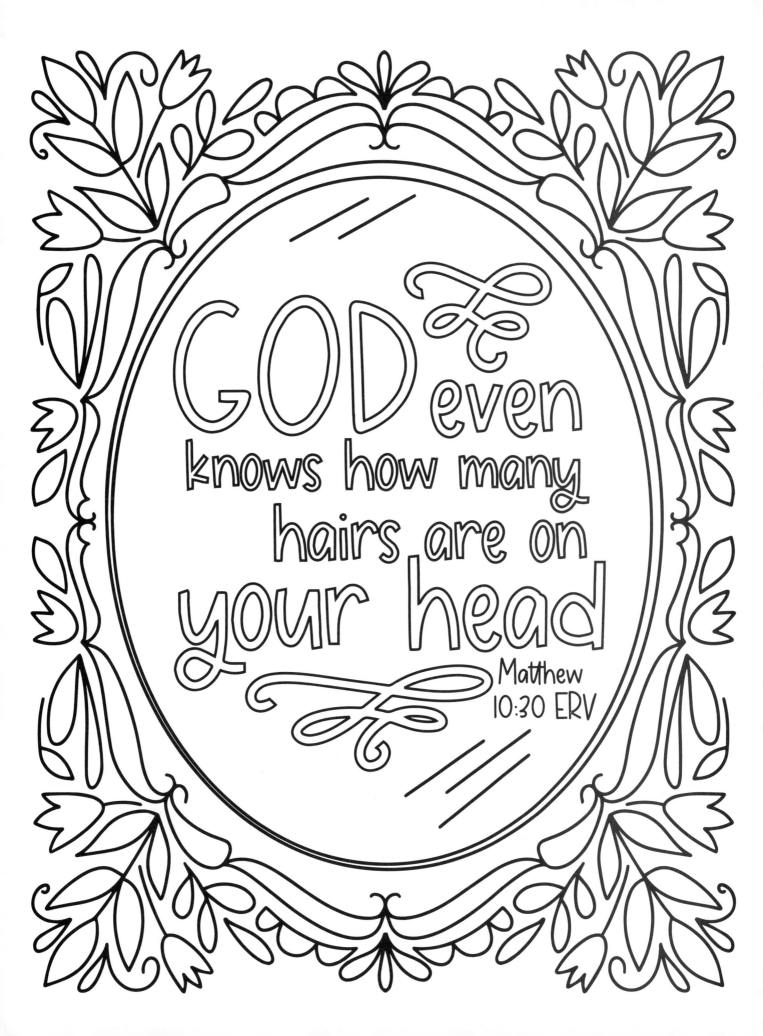

GOD even knows how many hairs are on your head

Matthew 10:30 ERV

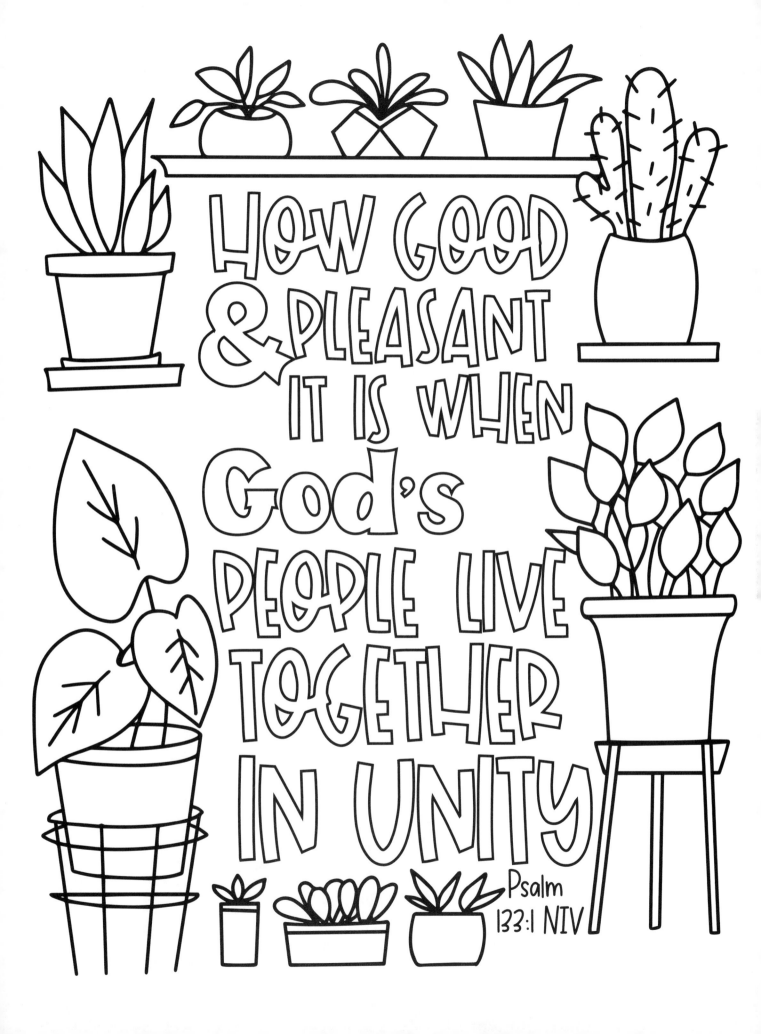

How Good & Pleasant it is when God's People Live Together in Unity

Psalm 133:1 NIV

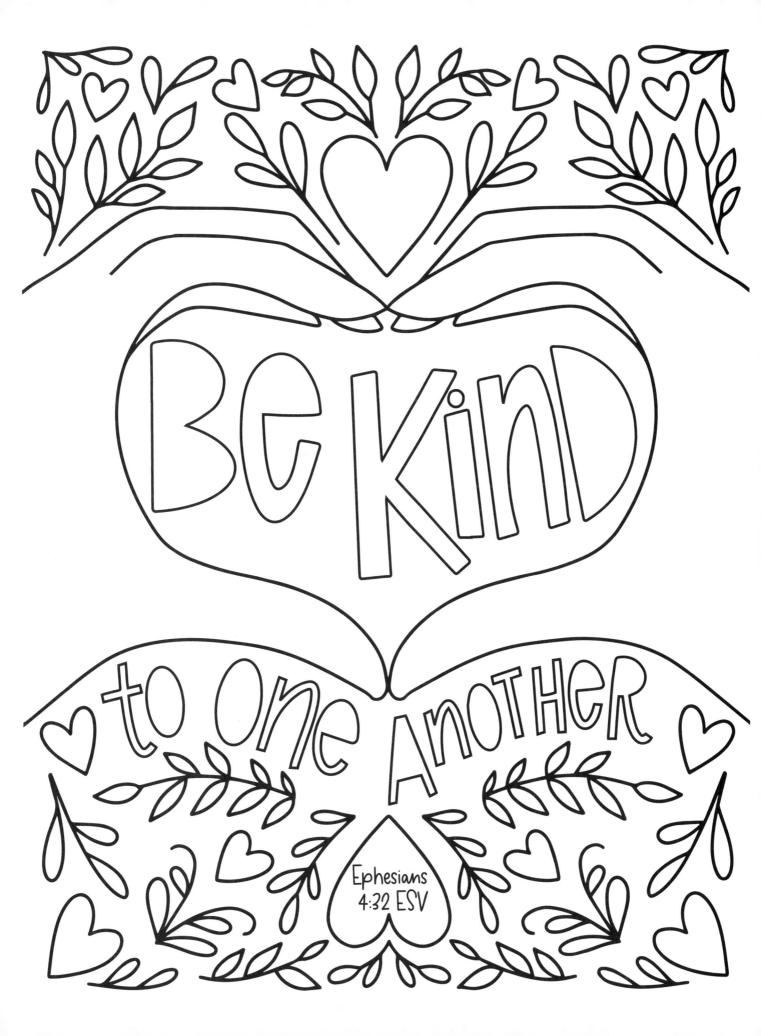

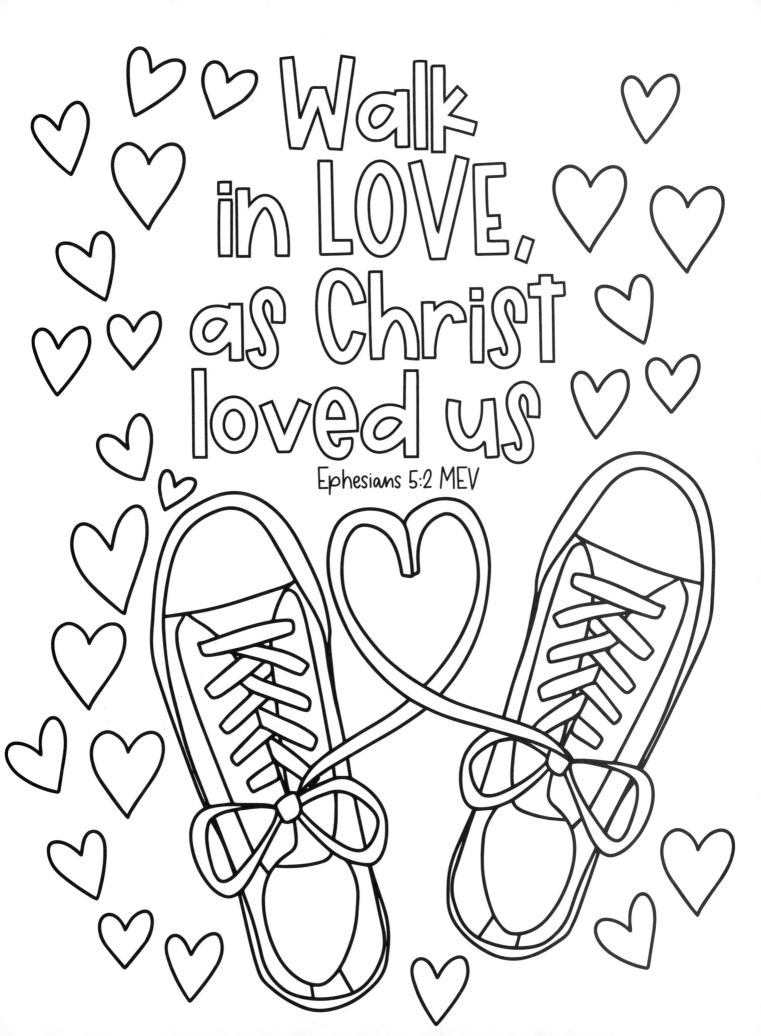

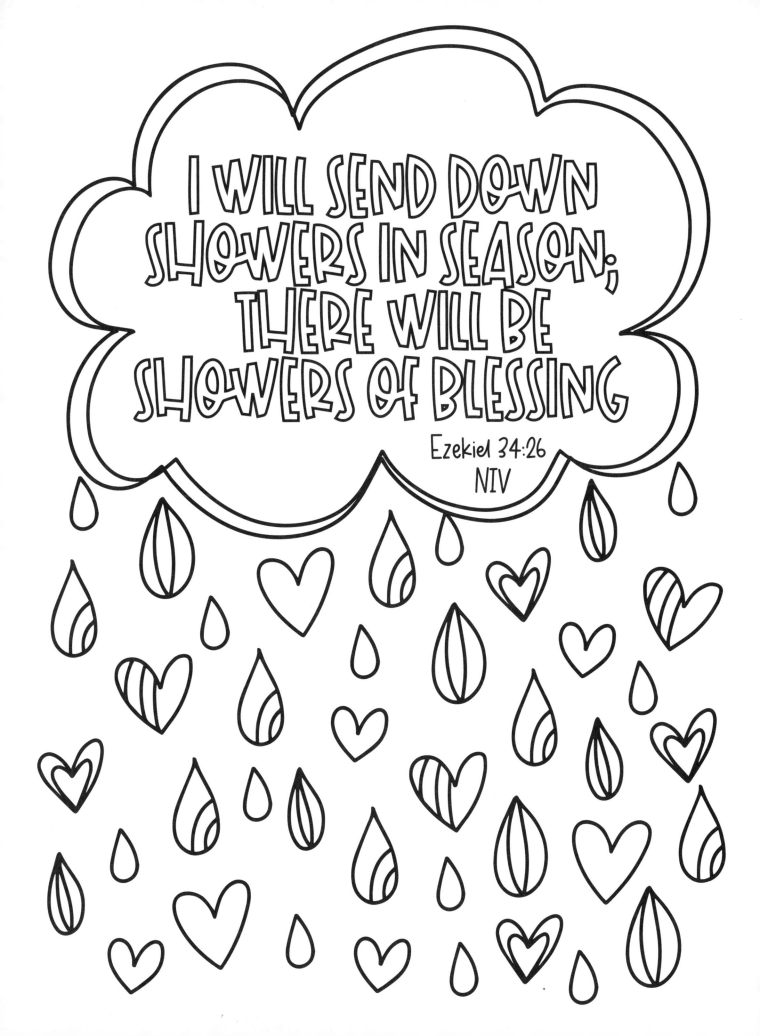

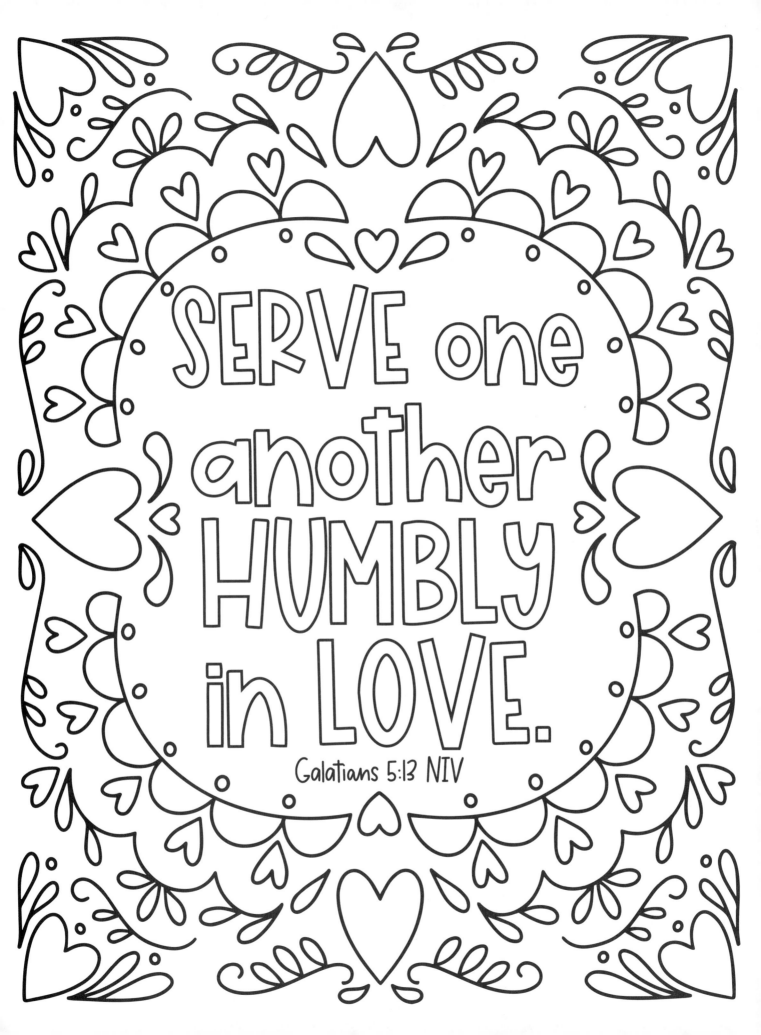

SERVE one another HUMBLY in LOVE.

Galatians 5:13 NIV

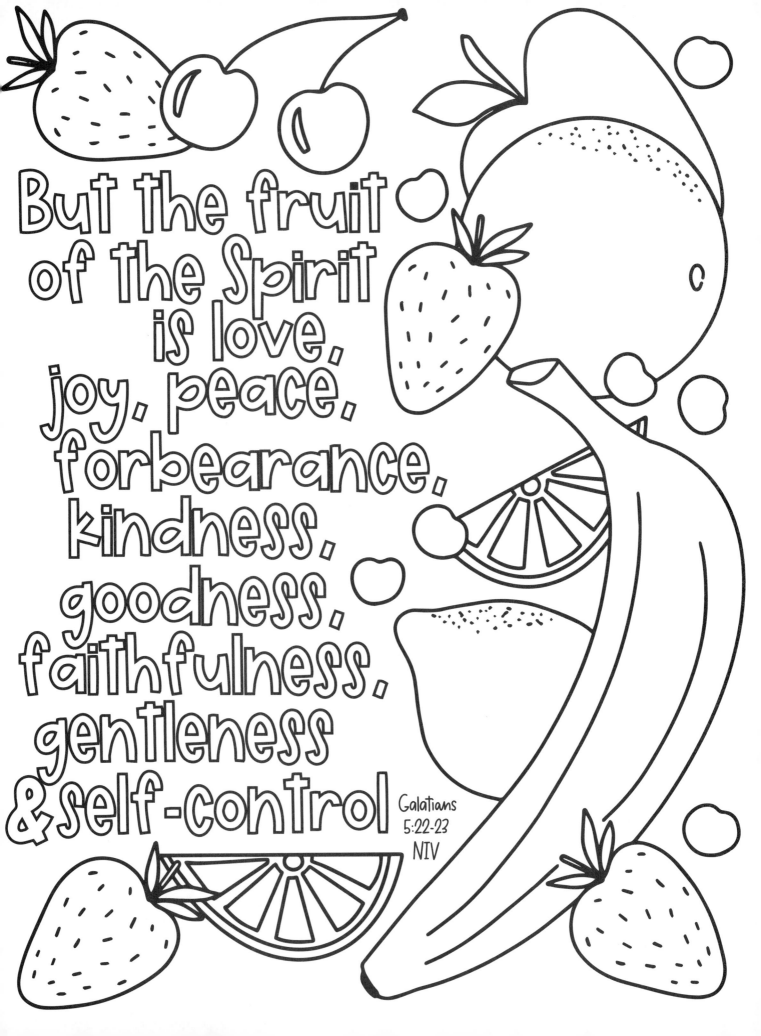

But the fruit of the Spirit is love, joy, peace, forbearance, kindness, goodness, faithfulness, gentleness & self-control

Galatians 5:22-23 NIV

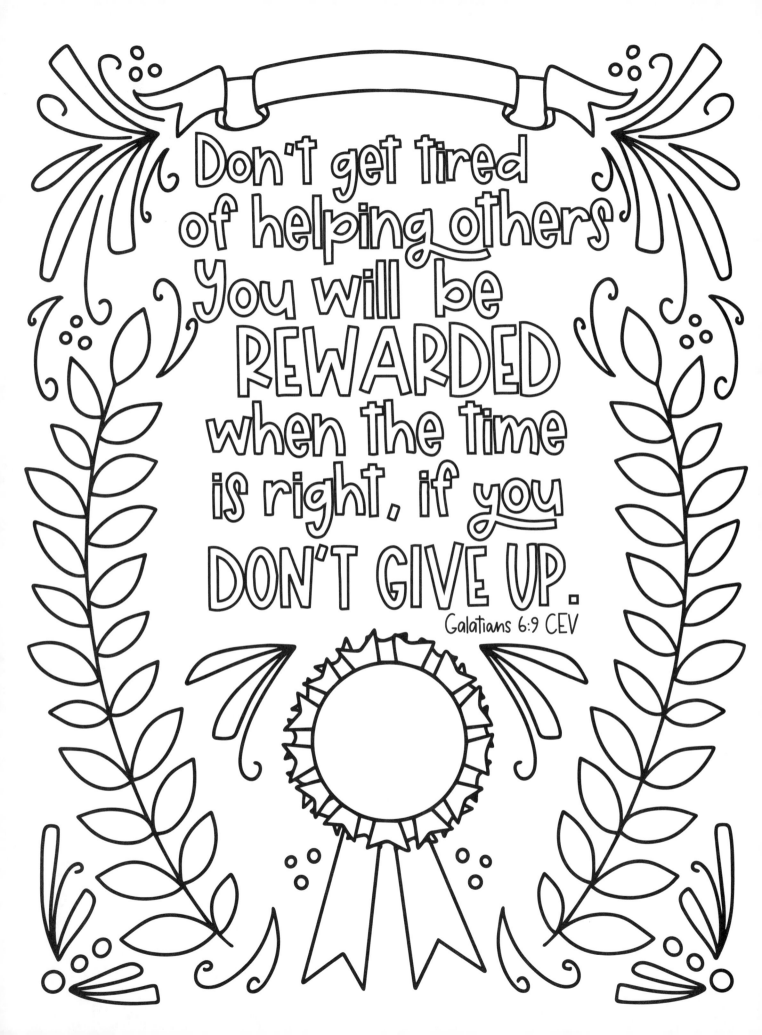

Don't get tired of helping others. You will be REWARDED when the time is right, if you DON'T GIVE UP.

Galatians 6:9 CEV

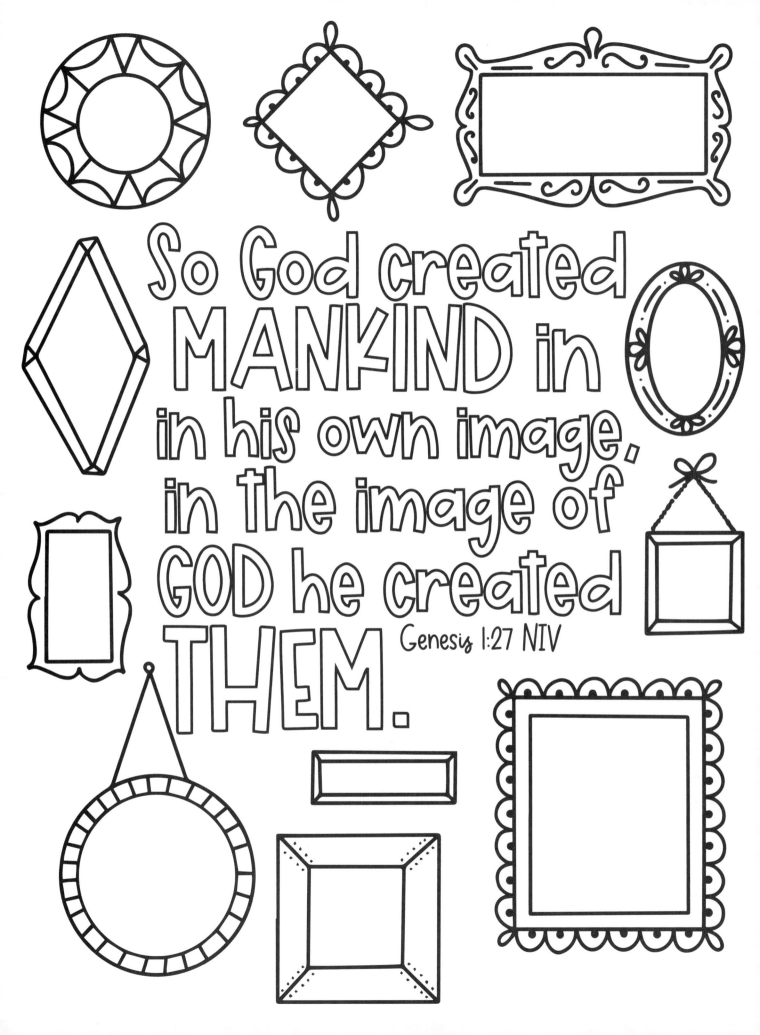

So God created MANKIND in in his own image, in the image of GOD he created THEM.

Genesis 1:27 NIV

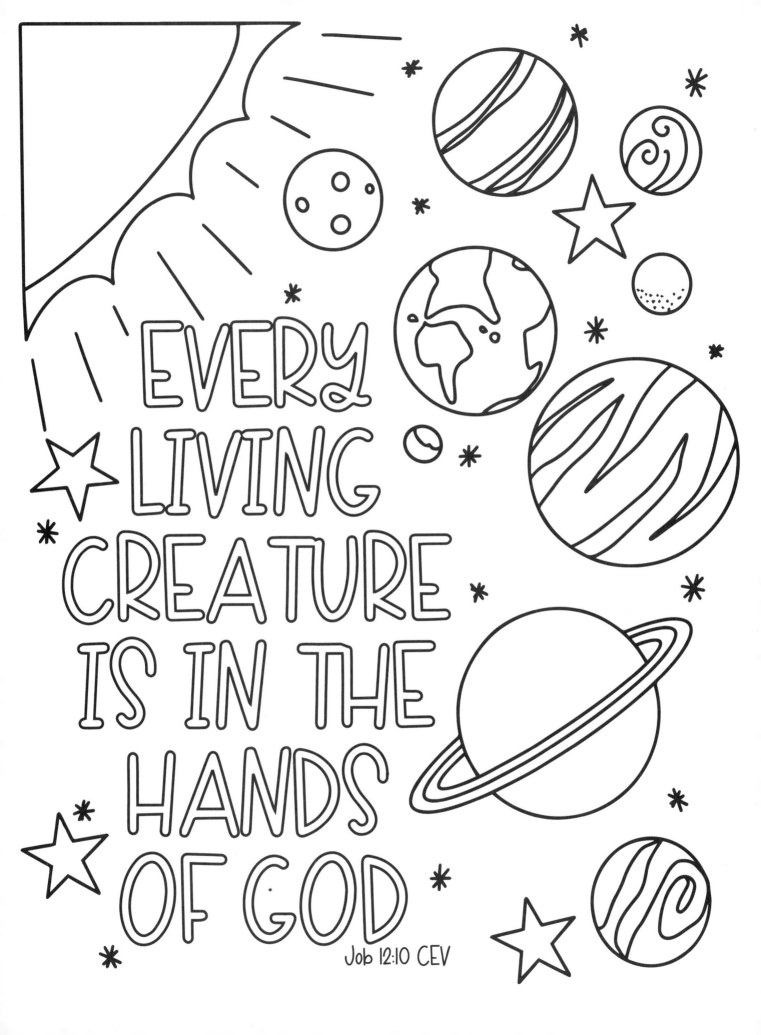

EVERY LIVING CREATURE IS IN THE HANDS OF GOD

Job 12:10 CEV

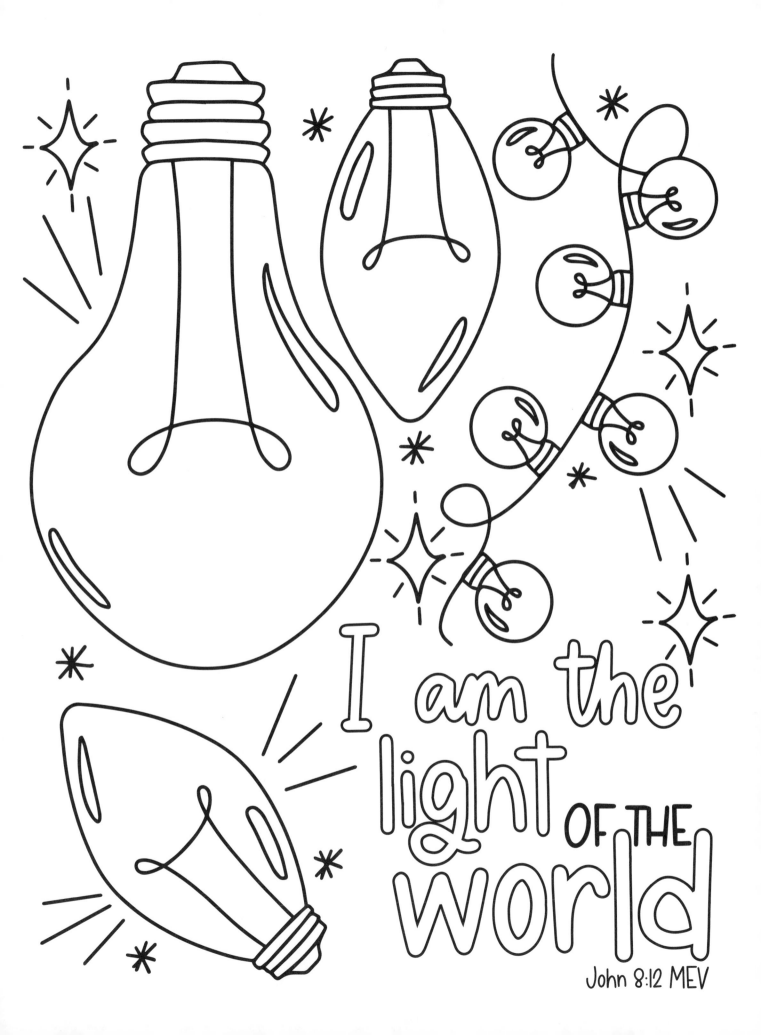

I am the
light
OF THE
world

John 8:12 MEV

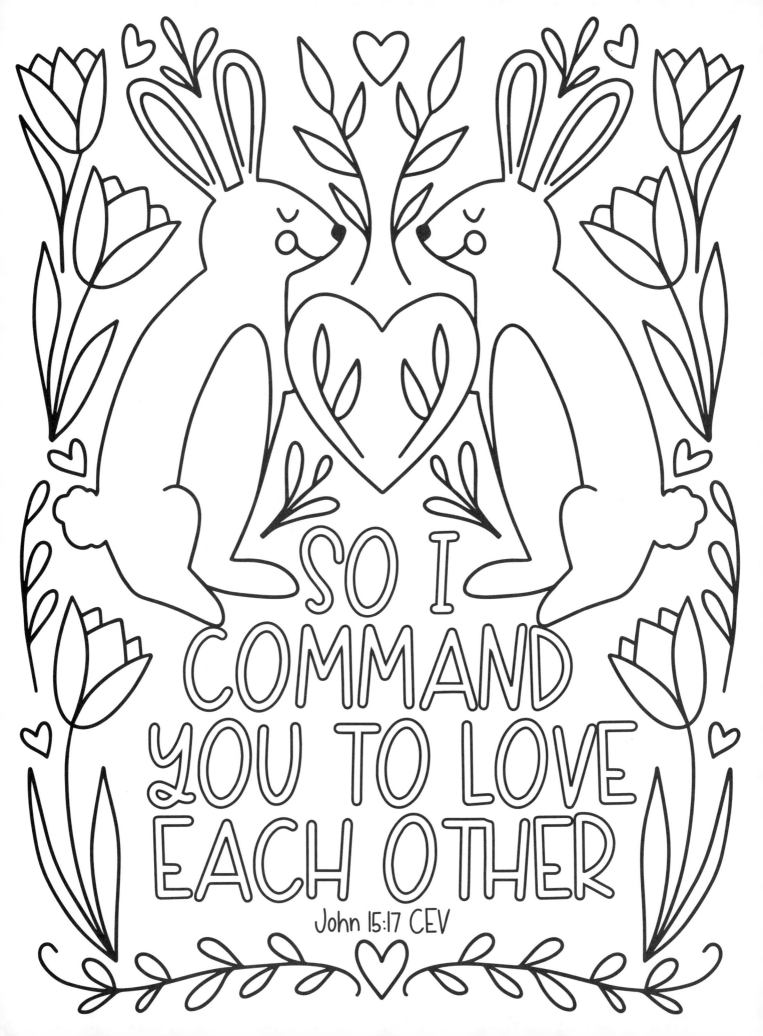

The Lord your God is with you wherever you go

Joshua 1:9 MEV

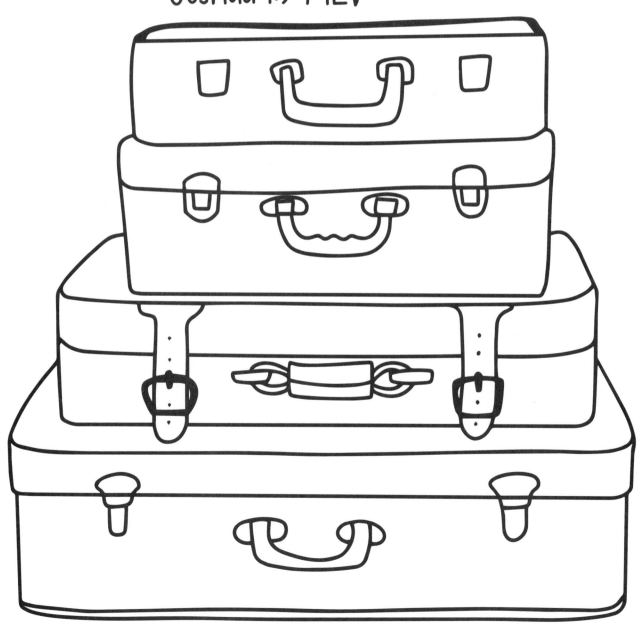

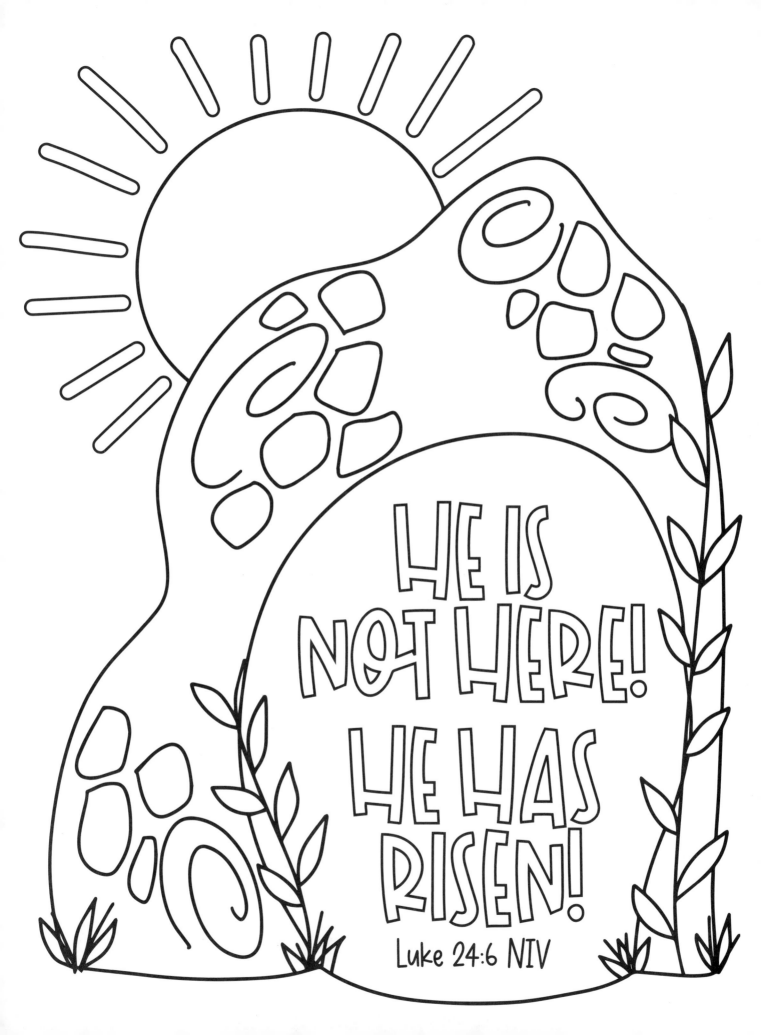

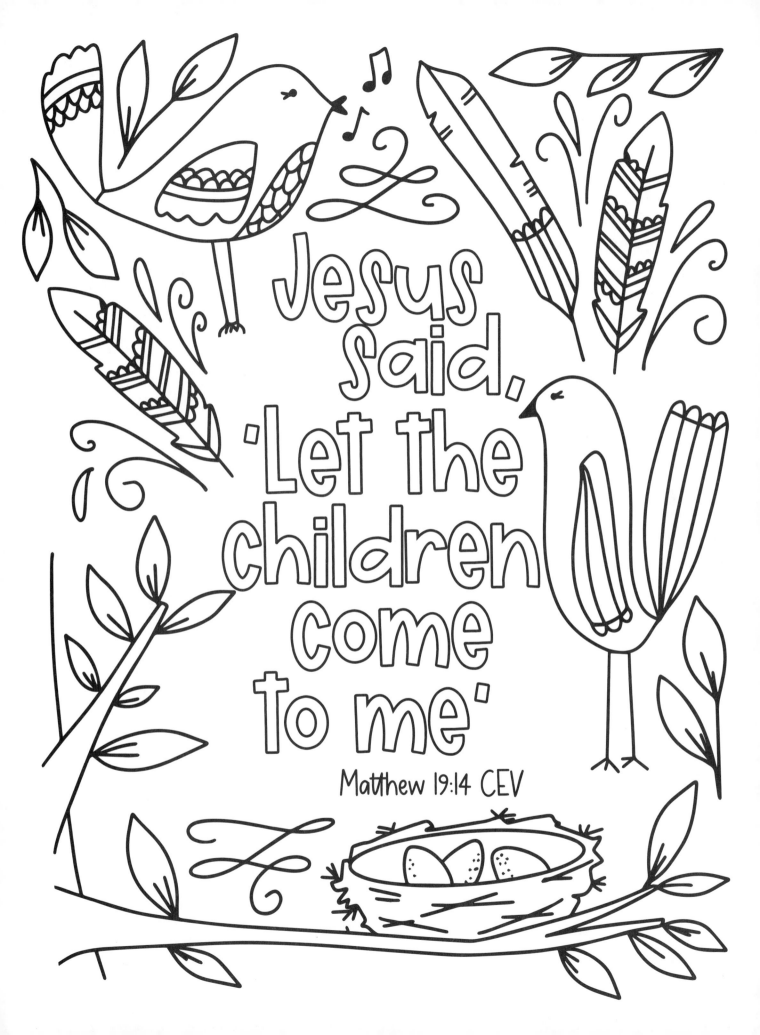

Jesus said, 'Let the children come to me'

Matthew 19:14 CEV

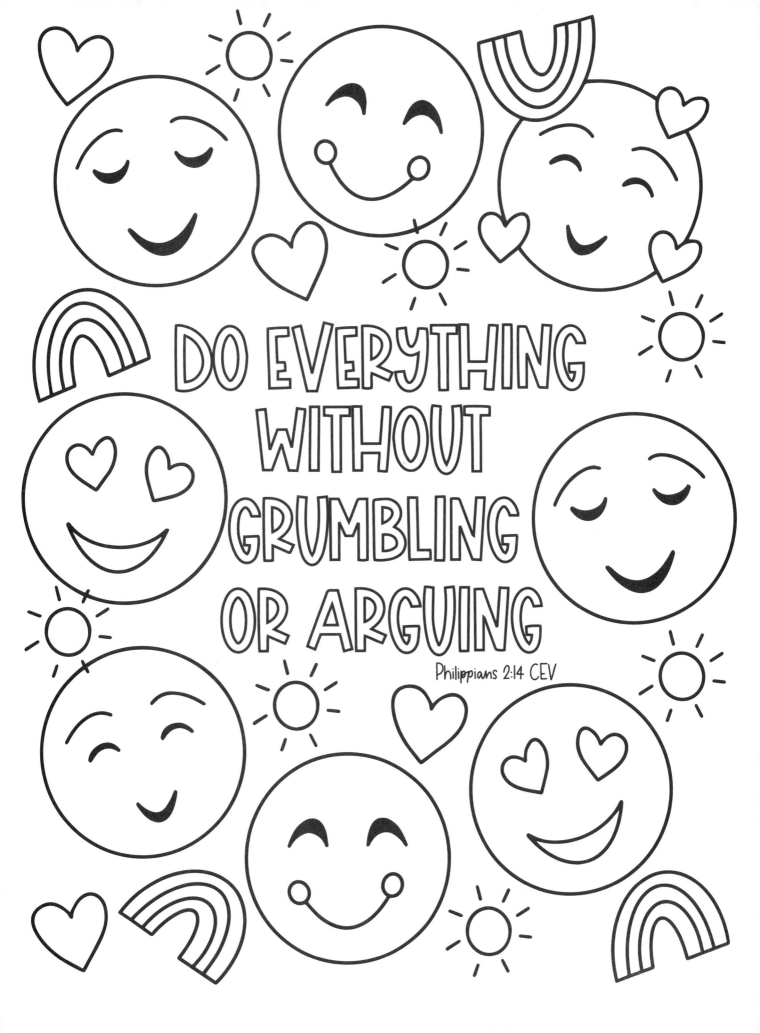

DO EVERYTHING WITHOUT GRUMBLING OR ARGUING

Philippians 2:14 CEV

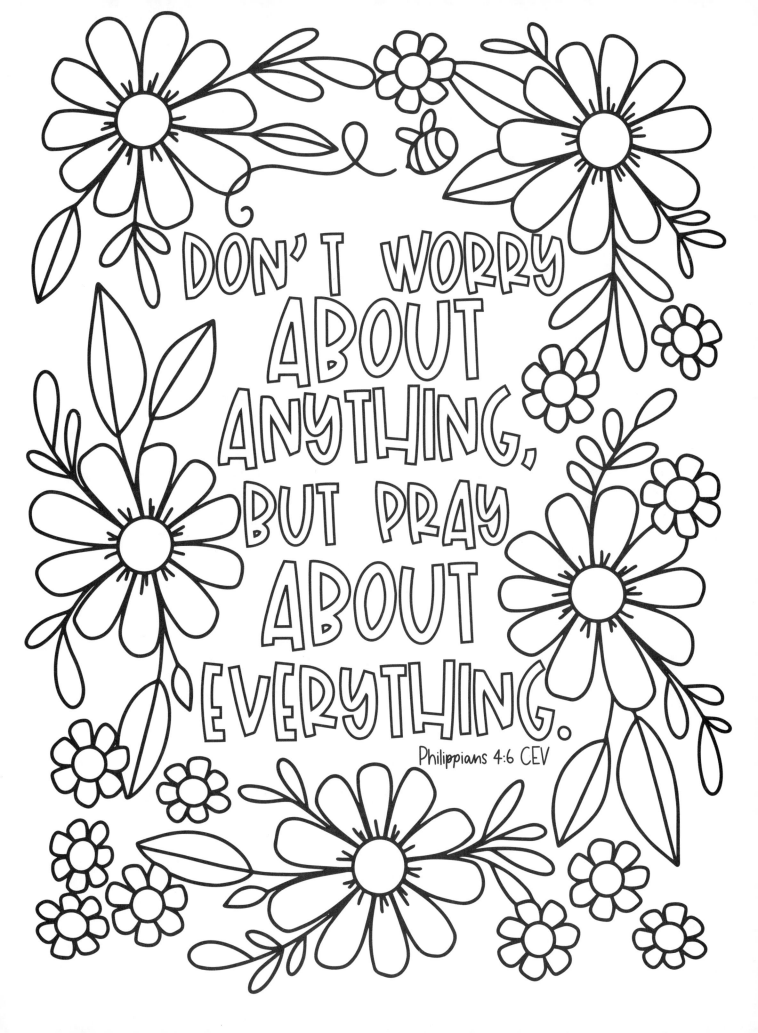

Don't worry about anything, but pray about everything.

Philippians 4:6 CEV

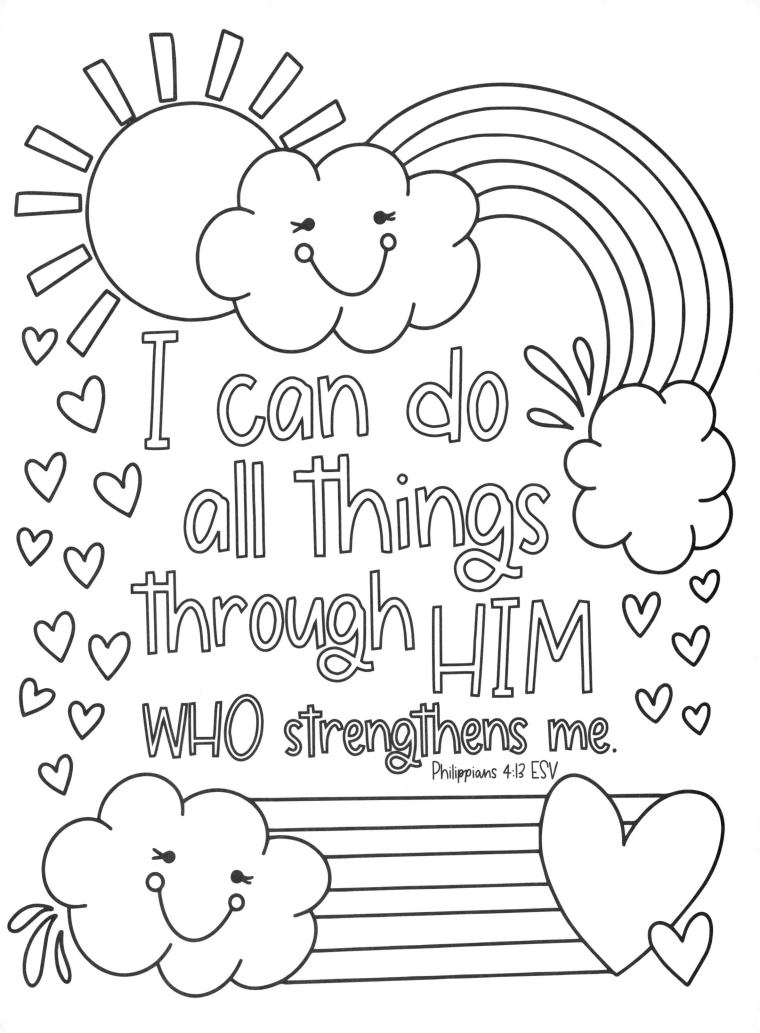

I can do all things through HIM WHO strengthens me.
Philippians 4:13 ESV

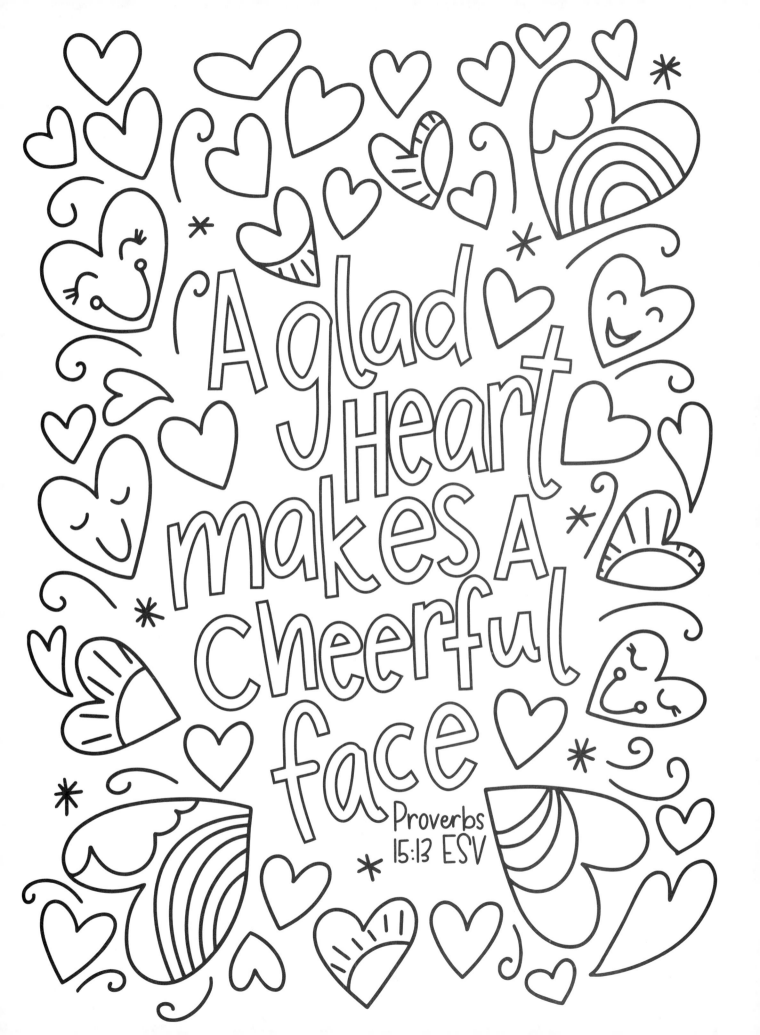

A glad Heart makes A Cheerful face

Proverbs 15:13 ESV

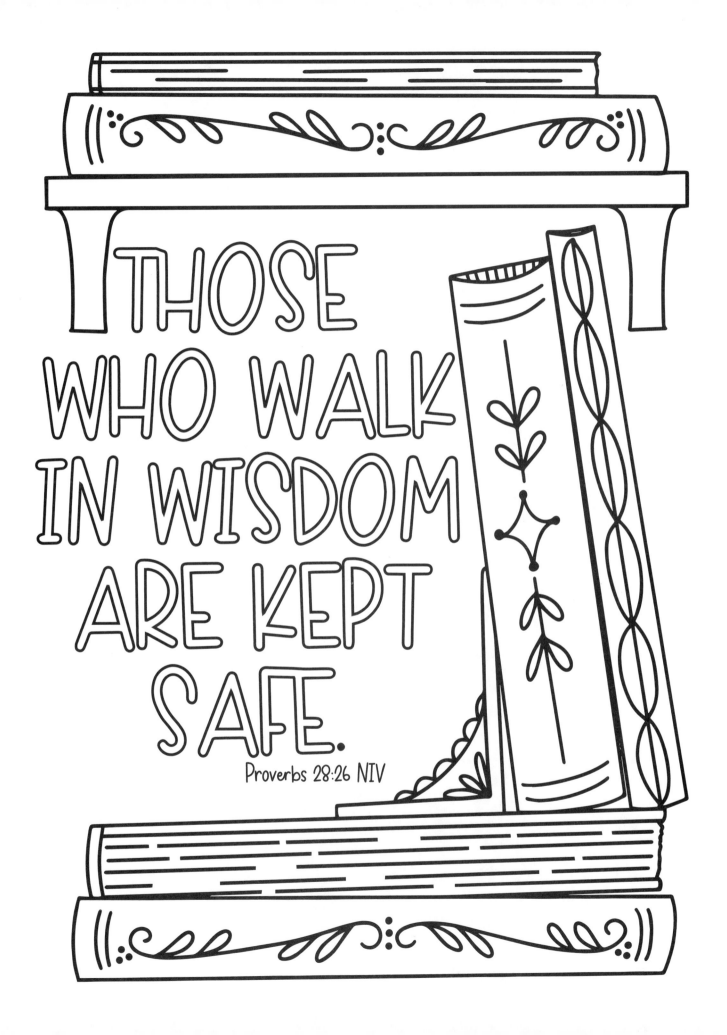

THOSE WHO WALK IN WISDOM ARE KEPT SAFE.

Proverbs 28:26 NIV

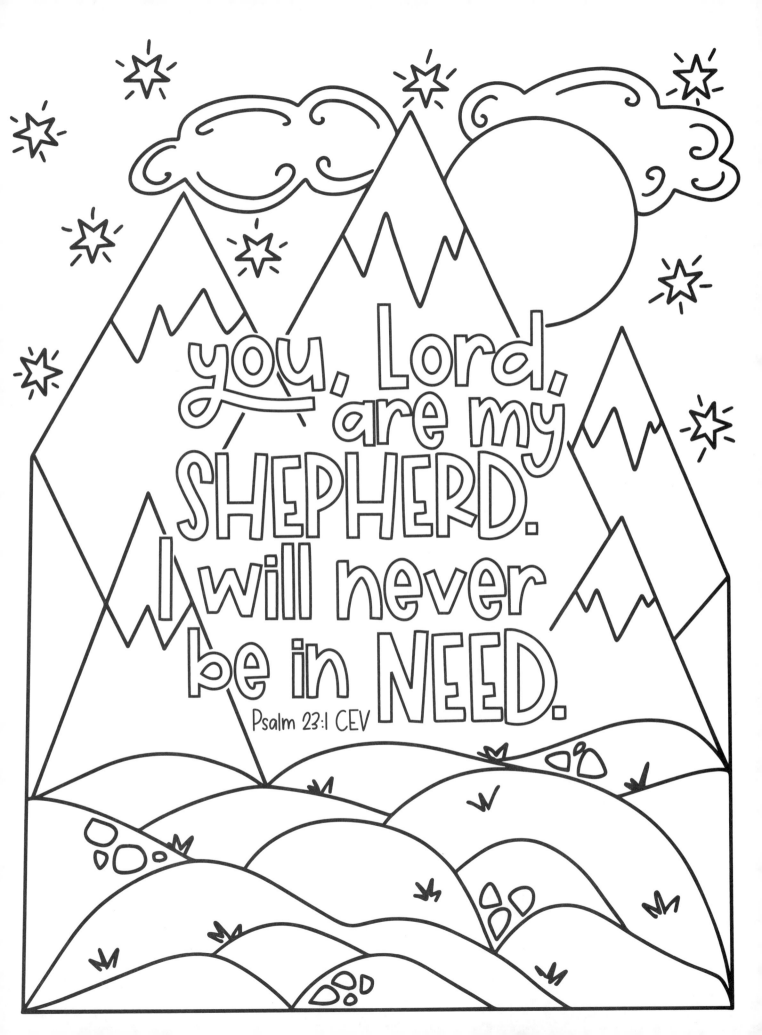

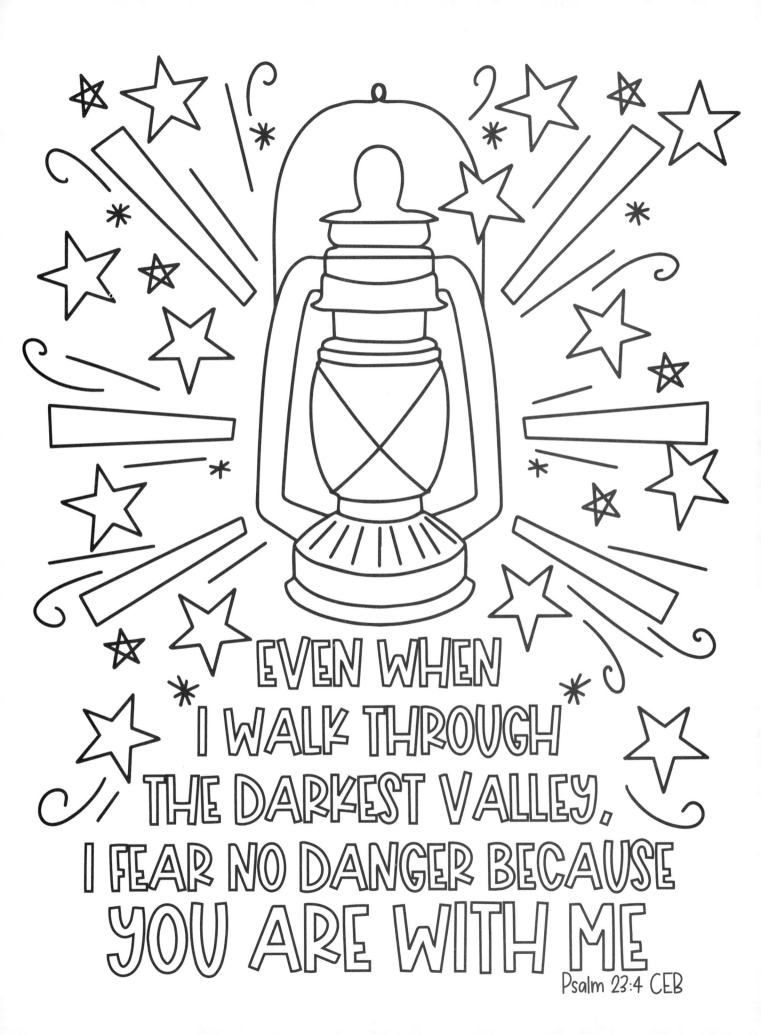

EVEN WHEN
I WALK THROUGH
THE DARKEST VALLEY,
I FEAR NO DANGER BECAUSE
YOU ARE WITH ME

Psalm 23:4 CEB

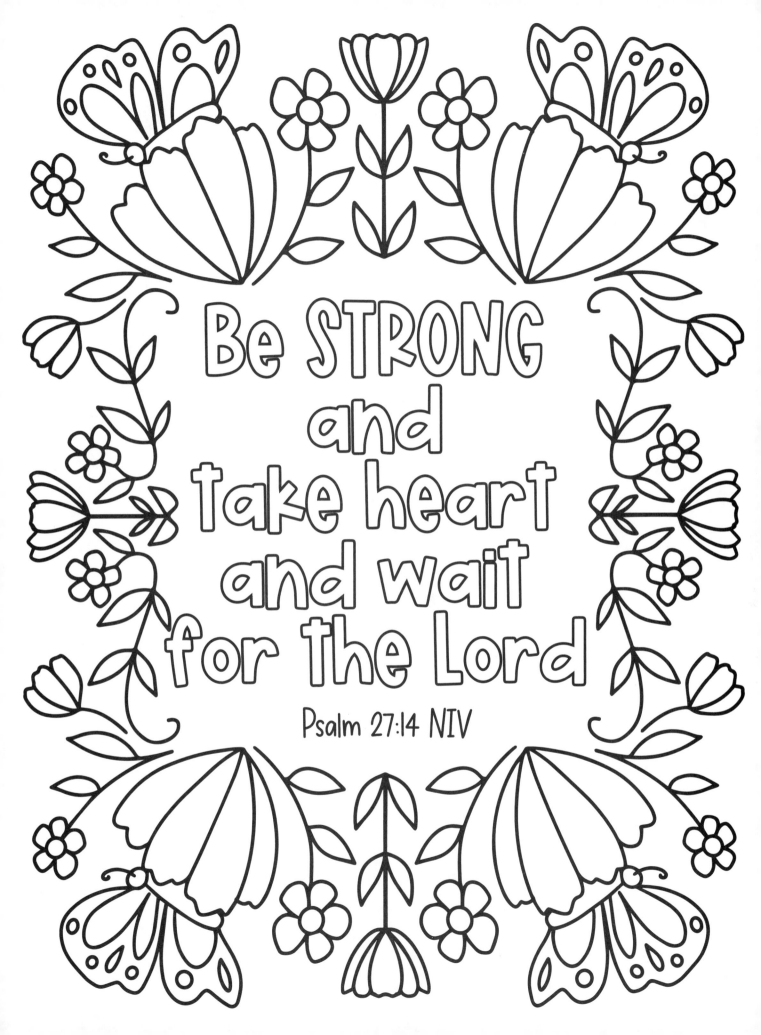

Be STRONG and take heart and wait for the Lord

Psalm 27:14 NIV

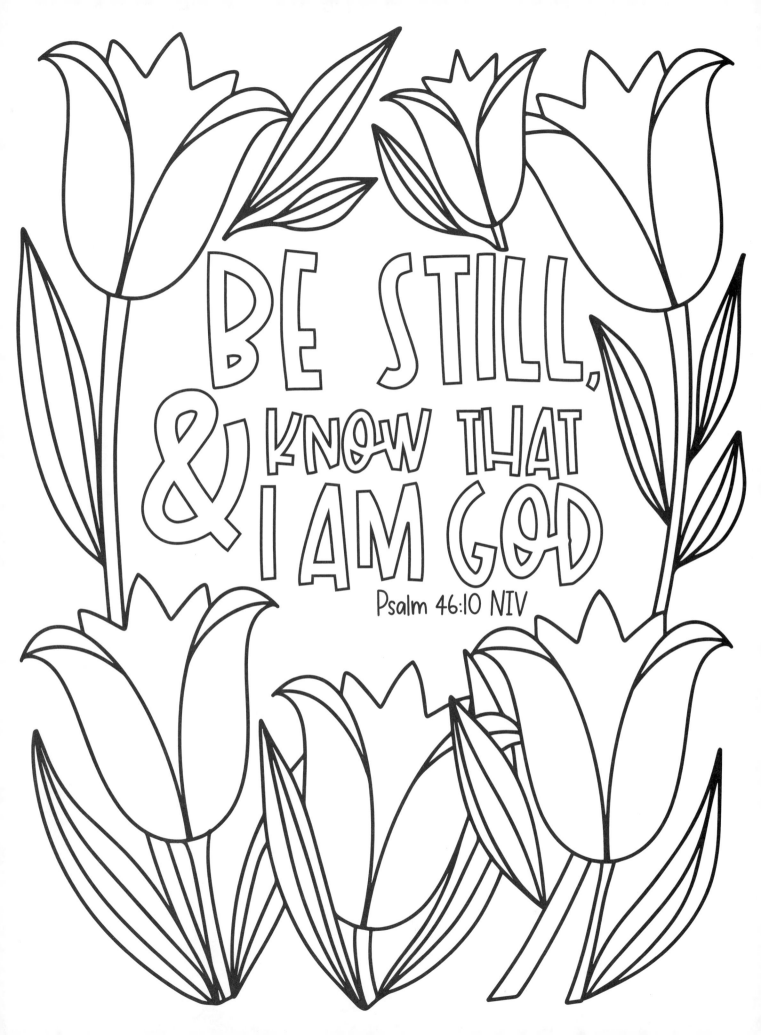

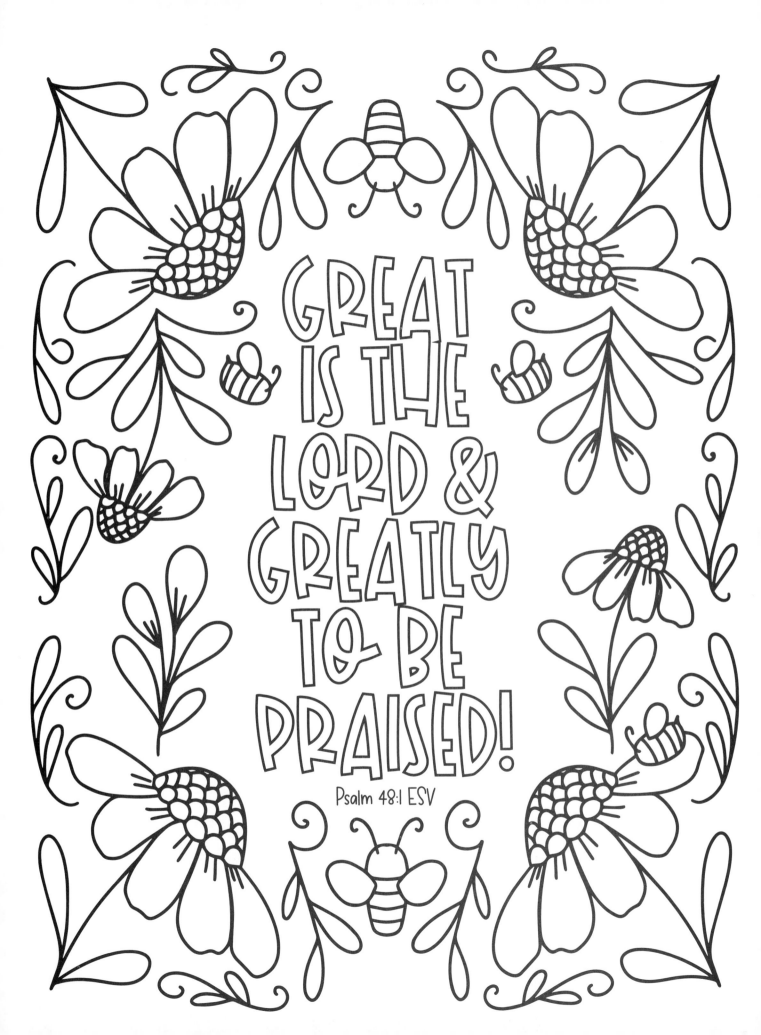

GREAT IS THE LORD & GREATLY TO BE PRAISED!

Psalm 48:1 ESV

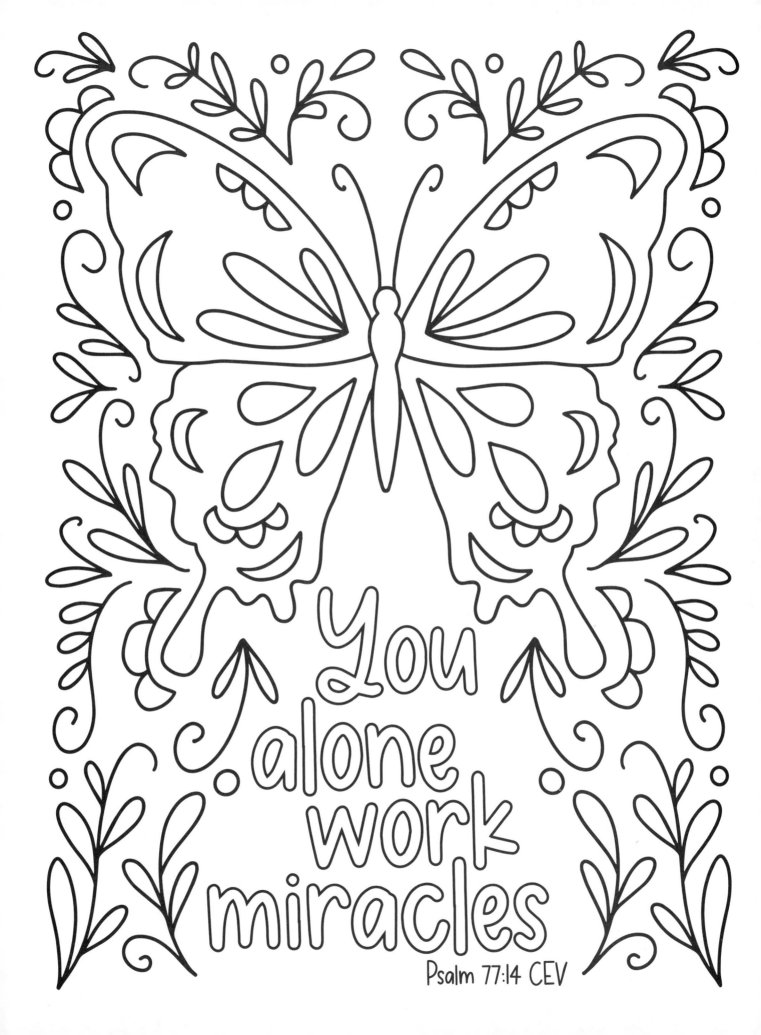

You alone work miracles

Psalm 77:14 CEV

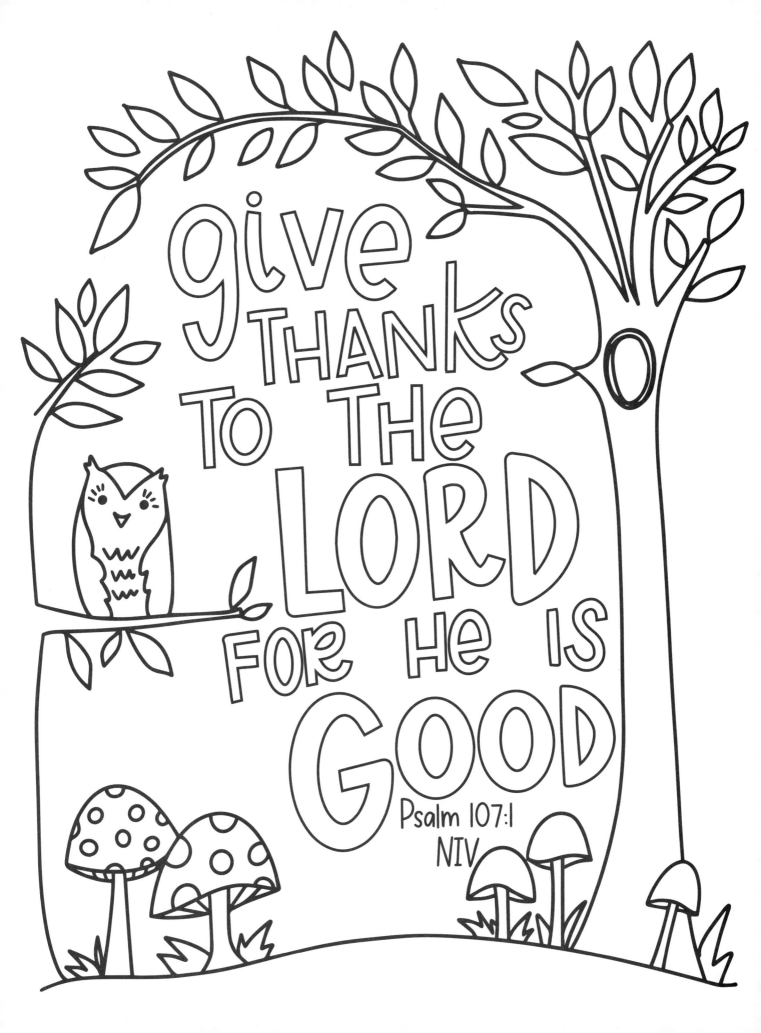

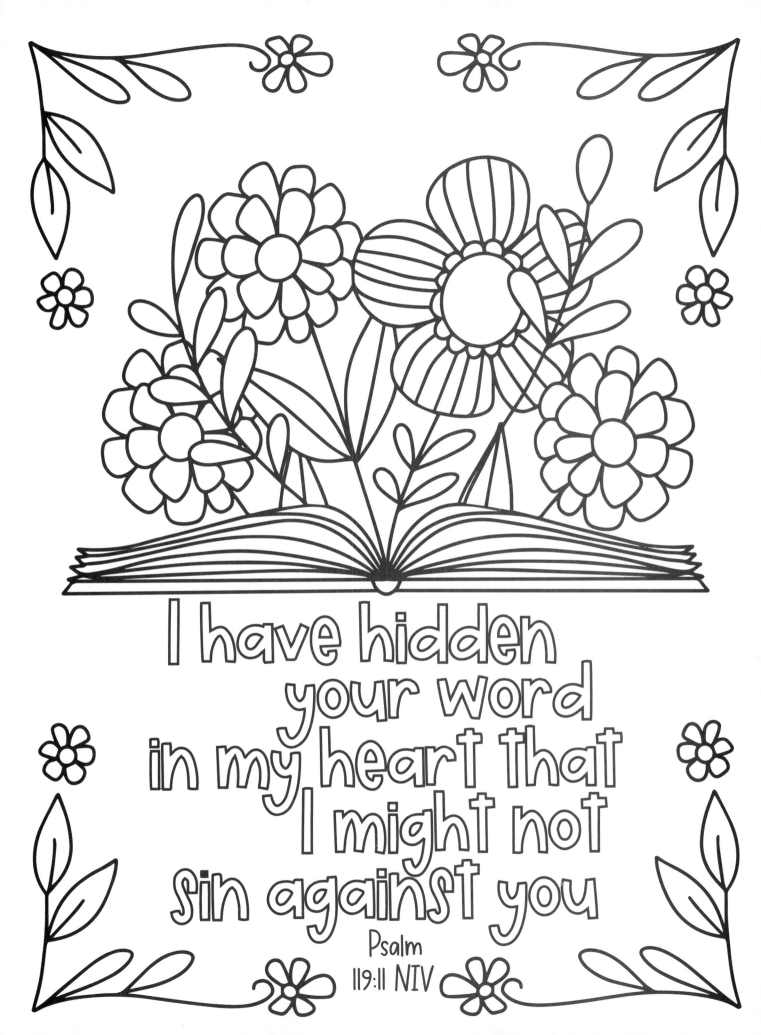

I have hidden
your word
in my heart that
I might not
sin against you

Psalm
119:11 NIV

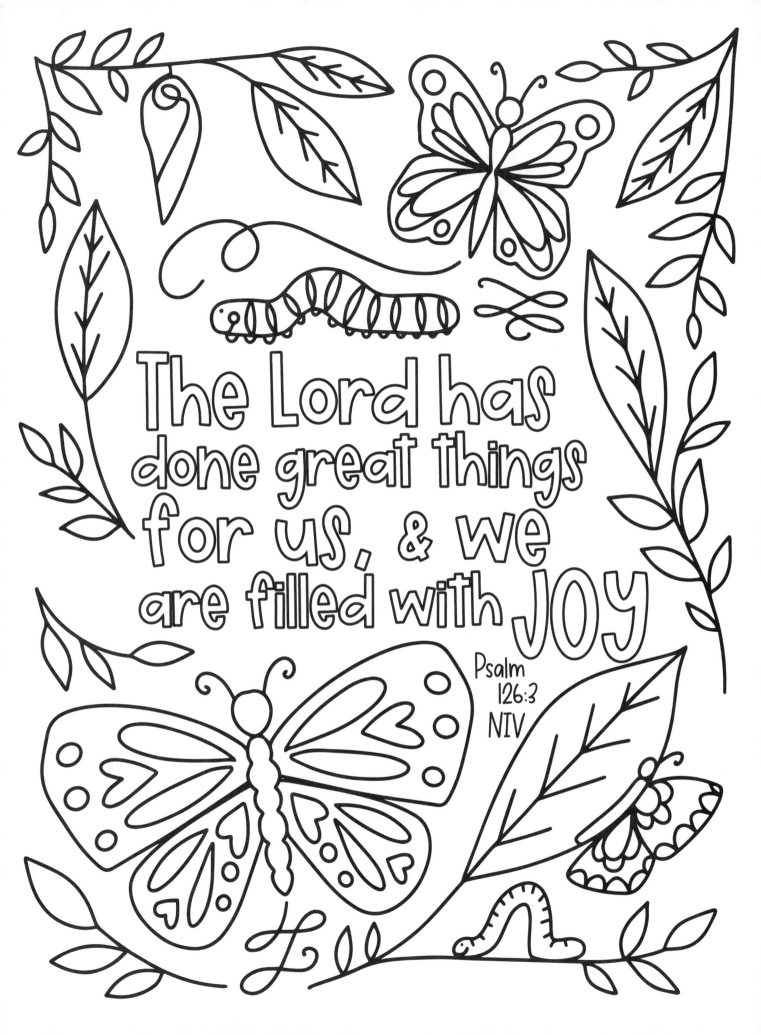

The Lord has done great things for us, & we are filled with JOY

Psalm 126:3 NIV

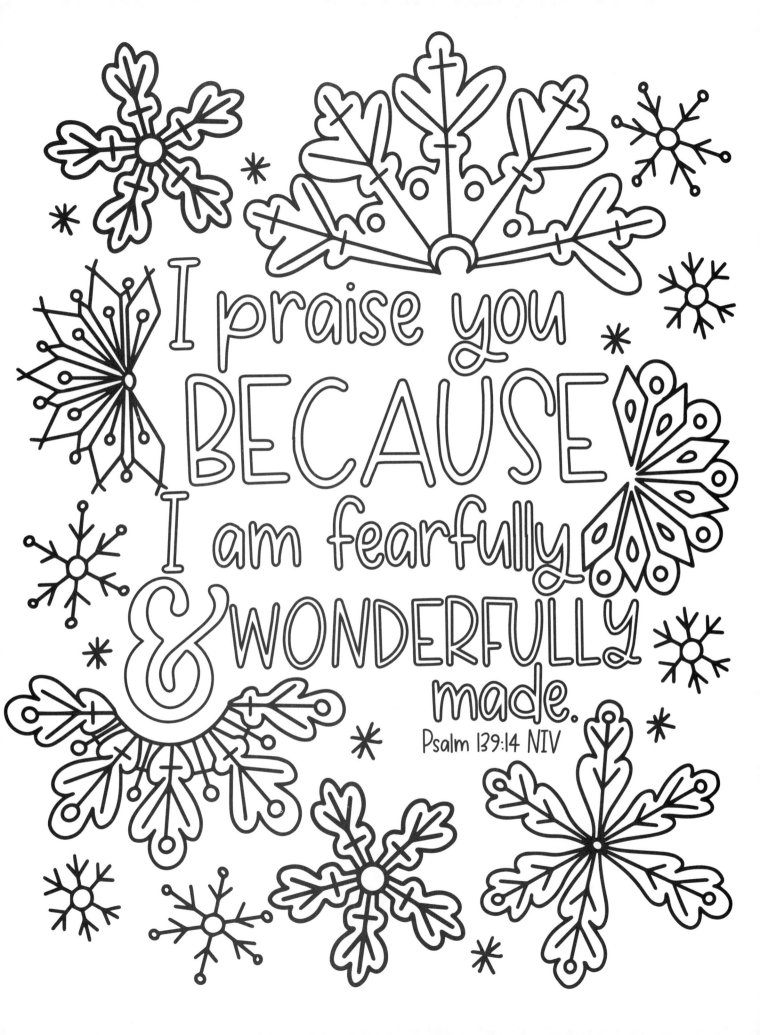

I praise you BECAUSE I am fearfully & WONDERFULLY made.

Psalm 139:14 NIV

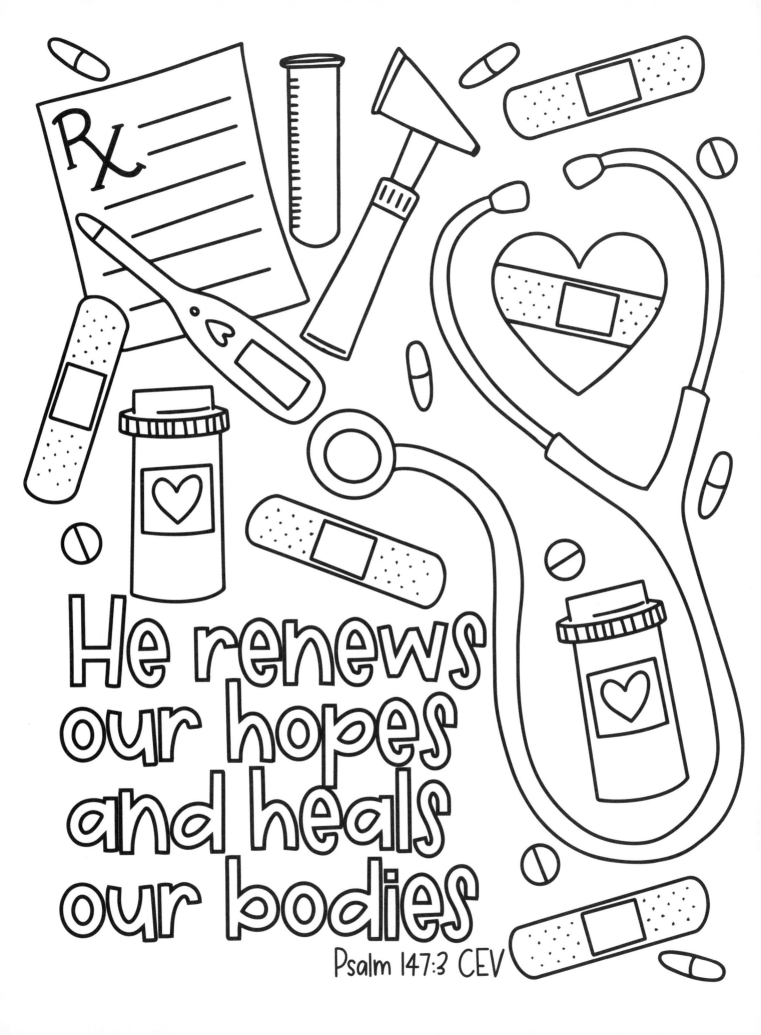

He renews
our hopes
and heals
our bodies

Psalm 147:3 CEV

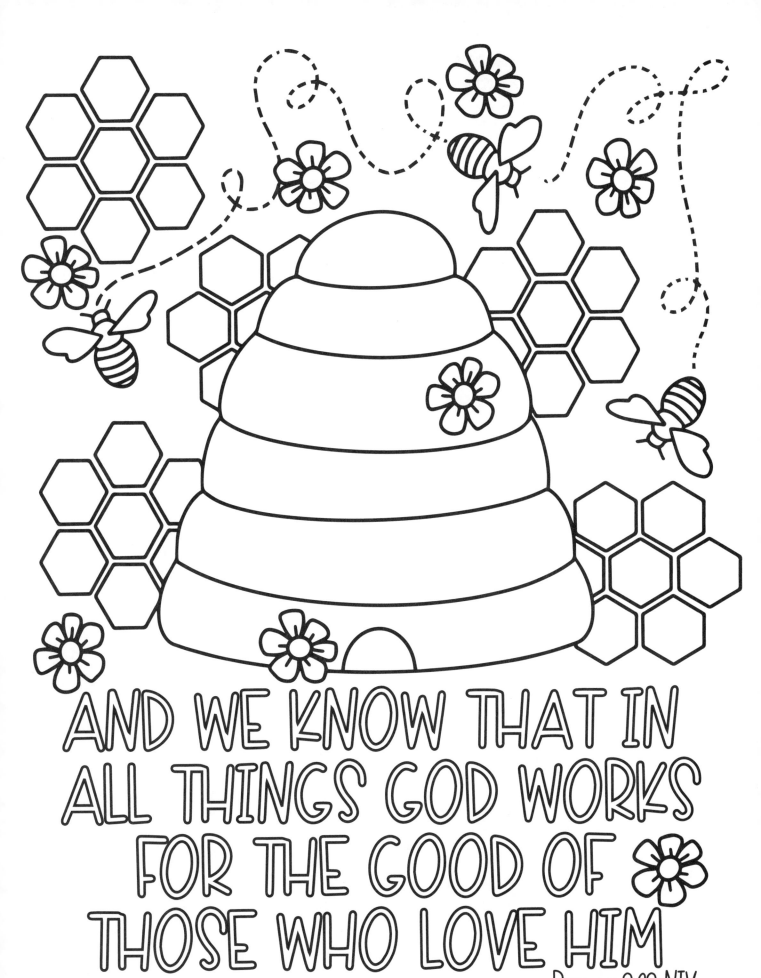

AND WE KNOW THAT IN
ALL THINGS GOD WORKS
FOR THE GOOD OF
THOSE WHO LOVE HIM
Romans 8:28 NIV

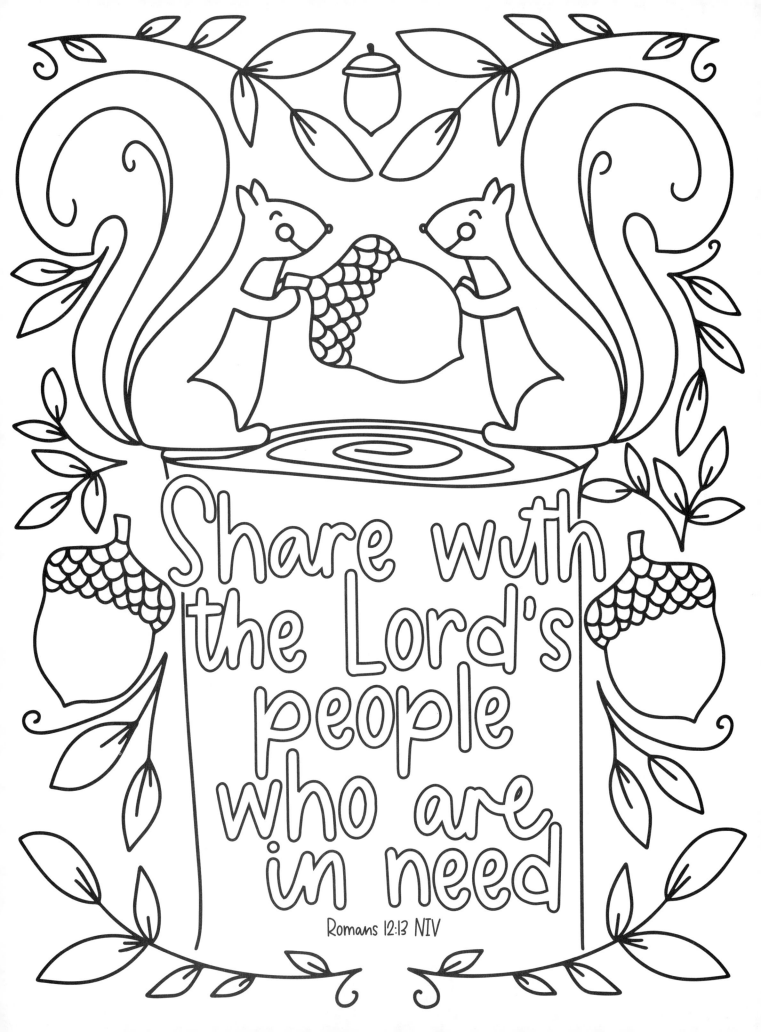

Share with the Lord's people who are in need

Romans 12:13 NIV

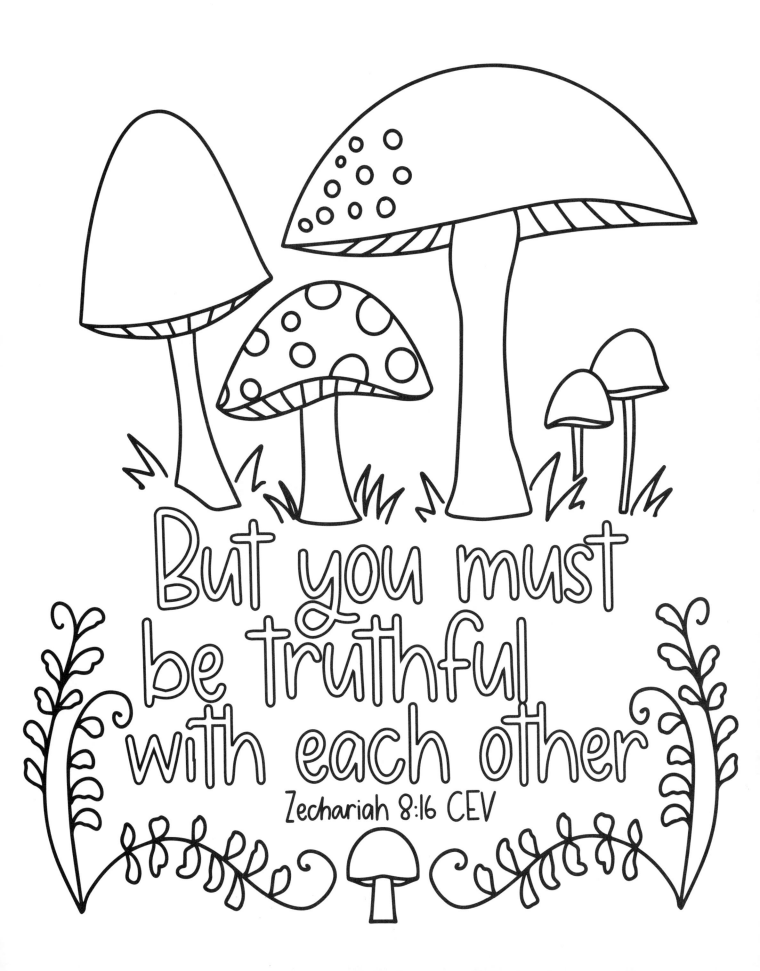

But you must
be truthful
with each other

Zechariah 8:16 CEV

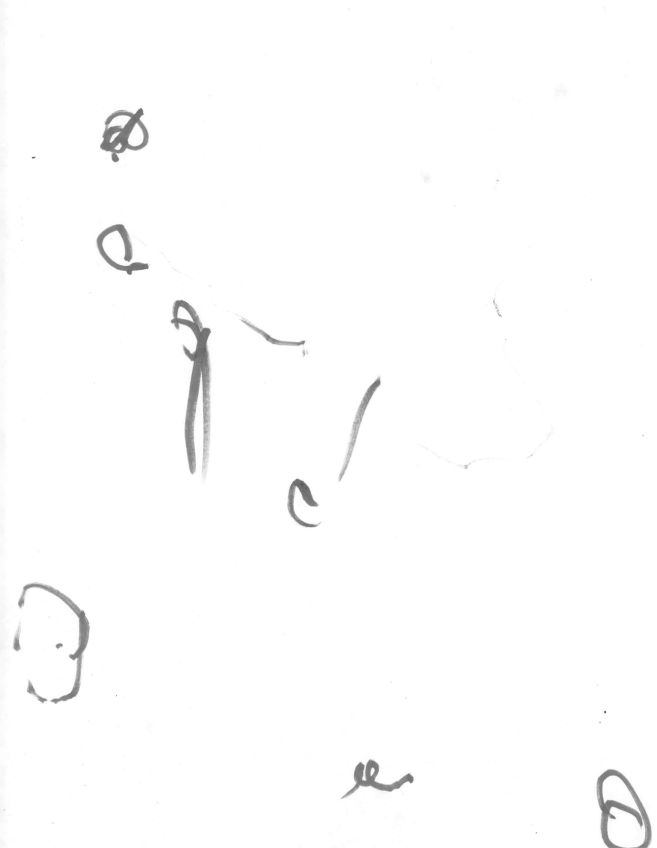